The

A Pilgrim's Companion
to Paray-le-Monial

by
David Baldwin

*All booklets are published thanks to the
generous support of the members of the
Catholic Truth Society*

CATHOLIC TRUTH SOCIETY
PUBLISHERS TO THE HOLY SEE

Contents

People, places and history 3

Saint Margaret Mary Alacoque 11

Saint Claude de la Colombière 27

The Basilica of the Sacred Heart 32

Chapel of the Visitation 45

Adoration Chapel of Saint John 51

Chapelle la Colombière 57

Final thoughts 65

*Most Sacred Heart of Jesus,
we place all our trust in You*

People, places and history

"The term 'Sacred Heart of Jesus' denotes the entire mystery of Christ, the totality of His being and His person …. Devotion to the Sacred Heart is a wonderful historical expression of the Church's piety for Christ … it calls for a fundamental attitude of conversion and reparation, of love and gratitude, apostolic commitment and dedication to Christ and His saving work" (Directory on Popular Piety and the Liturgy).

Devotion to the Sacred Heart of Jesus in the Catholic Church runs long and deep. In many Catholic churches – maybe all – you will invariably see the familiar image of the Sacred Heart, maybe by picture, but usually by statue, or sometimes at a side chapel or altar, of Jesus, with His Heart exposed at His chest, usually aflame and surrounded by the crown of thorns, sometimes held in His hand. Many households, in many countries, may display a picture or small statue; when abroad, you may also come across a street niche sheltering the statue.

Long tradition

It is a sentiment that has been expressed in some form from the earliest times – through St Augustine

(354–430), St Bernard (c1090–1153) and St Catherine of Siena (1347–1380). The mystic and visionary St Gertrude (1256–1302) prophesied that the secrets of the Sacred Heart would be revealed at a later age when love for God had grown cold and weak. It started emerging in the Middle Ages with a bit more coherence when the faithful specifically wished to recall Jesus' unfailing love through giving His life on the Cross, and which, as He recounted from the Scriptures, "from his heart shall flow streams of living water" (*Jn* 7:38). And from that pierced side, "immediately there came out blood and water" (*Jn* 19:34), about which the Fathers of the Church have taught us that the Holy Spirit flowed upon the Church.

The French priest, St John Eudes (1601–1680), started formulating and propagating a specific devotion through his *Office of the Sacred Heart*, winning recognition from Pope St Pius X as the Father of Worship to the Sacred Heart (and Immaculate Heart of Mary), and declaring him the Apostle and Doctor of these devotions.

Margaret Mary

However, it was only when, through the revelations and specific instructions of Our Lord to Sister Margaret Mary Alacoque (1647–1690), a nun in her convent in the depths of rural France at Paray-le-Monial, and assisted by the convent chaplain, St Claude de la Colombière

(1641–1682), that the devotion spread and took hold universally. It may be held that this particular devotion came just at the right moment – France had been devastated by nearly a century of religious and civil wars, and religion at the time is described as being a cold, joyless, formulaic affair.

Today, particularly with the younger generations, and with the onset of other more recent devotions such as the Divine Mercy and the rejuvenation of the rosary with the institution of the Luminous Mysteries by Pope John Paul II, it may be that this devotion is gently slipping from sight. To my own chagrin – despite being familiar with the Sacred Heart – it had also receded from my horizon. It was only when seeking out the shrines of France that my travels took me to the small town of Paray-le-Monial, in southern Burgundy – recognised as the physical wellspring of the 'modern' devotion to the Sacred Heart – that renewed in me a recognition of the significance of this devotion, and a desire to fan again the flames surrounding that 'Precious Heart'.

Purpose of this book

This book has three purposes. Firstly, to describe the people and the places involved in this significant devotion, and so open it up to those who may not be aware, or only vaguely aware of this devotion. Its purpose is to help us all to contemplate what role this devotion can play in our life, and how we can address and implement it. For everybody it should also provide the added bonus of giving an 'appetiser' for a visit to Paray, or at very least, take you on an armchair pilgrimage!

It is also intended as a pilgrim's companion to help those who are specifically going to Paray on their pilgrimage, to immerse themselves in this powerful and peaceful wellspring of the Sacred Heart. It will briefly recount the stories of the people involved, take you to the principal pilgrim places of the modern genesis of this devotion, providing coherent commentary and narrative description as you go round, as well as suggesting appropriate prayers and meditations along the way.

Thirdly, for those of you intending to holiday in, or even just pass through this region, it may be worth slipping this small book in with your travel guides – a detour to this small, tranquil town and its sublime, holy places may provide a welcome and refreshing distraction from the frenecity of the tourist trail!

Paray-le-Monial

Paray-le-Monial is a small, relaxed, picturesque rural town of some 10,000 souls in the depths of southern Burgundy, about 100km northwest of Lyon. It is off the mainstream tourist trail, thus retaining its individual charm – as yet unblighted and unbranded by the 21st century's corporate outlets. Bisecting the town is the lazy-running river Bourbince, separating old from new. It is a town rightly proud of its extensive public gardens, small and large, in and around it – the principal one being the Parc du Moulin Liron, a 37 acre landscaped park, created for the visit of Pope John Paul II in October 1986, and displaying a large selection of trees and conifers from around the world. Apparently the town's only other claim to fame is that its inhabitants, in a siege about 1,000 years ago, were saved from starvation by *cacous*, their version of the fruit tart *clafouti*, made specifically with cherries, which grow in abundance in this region (recipe available at the Tourist Information Office)!

Despite its seeming anonymity, Paray is a significant place of pilgrimage, with devotees of the Sacred Heart coming from all corners of the earth. Up to 500,000 pilgrims come here over the year, so at times it may be busy in that sense – particularly on relevant feast days – but the spaces and places to cope with these numbers are there, whilst there are also many quiet spots for the pilgrim to seek out. Paray is twinned with the small cathedral city of Wells in Somerset (although Paray bears no comparison in size, being a lot smaller), and also, amongst others, with Bethlehem. It is an engaging, compact town – neat as a pin, partly pedestrianised, and easily walkable.

History

The town's more distant history is vested mainly in the arrival of the Benedictines, and the building and development of their first monastery church and community from 973 onwards. More recent history has made the town into a pilgrim venue. The Visitation nun, Margaret Mary Alacoque, whose mystic experiences and visions of Our Lord from 1673 to 1675 and subsequent promotion of devotion to the Sacred Heart of Jesus which brought her the crown of sainthood, also brought to her adopted town the responsibility of being the foremost shrine in the world, and the host for this devotion. The other principal person associated with St Margaret Mary and the Sacred Heart, was St Claude de la Colombière, a Jesuit priest and latterly chaplain to the Visitation sisters' community.

In putting this history into modern context, Pope John Paul II commented, in his homily on the Canonisation of St Claude de la Colombière in 1992: "In the 17th century the Lord chose your town to bring forth a new source of merciful and infinitely generous love on which generations of pilgrims would draw. The fecundity of grace attached to the cult of the Sacred Heart is especially manifest in the development of pilgrimages to Paray over the past few years. The diocese and the different communities present have helped bring many people to share in the wealth of the message entrusted to the Saints of your town".

Places

The principal pilgrim places in Paray associated with the Sacred Heart and these two saints are the striking and harmonious 11th century Romanesque Basilica of the Sacred Heart; the small, prayerful convent Chapel of the Visitation; and the arresting 20th century chapel commemorating St Claude de la Colombière. There are also some pilgrim 'extras': a simple barn-styled Adoration Chapel of St John, and the 'green cathedral', all set in the very agreeable context of this small town.

There is certainly a day's worth of 'pilgrimaging' to thoroughly and gently explore and experience all that is on offer here, and, if you want to extend your stay, there is very reasonable – in quality and price – religious and pilgrim accommodation, as well as the expected hotels and *auberges*. It is also on the main-line railway system. Paray is not overwhelmed with the plethora of devotional shops that encircle the sanctuary at Lourdes – it is all very low key and discreet. There are plenty of liturgical and devotional events going on at all these places throughout the day – details and timings can be obtained from the Pilgrim Information Office. The new movement, Emmanuel Community, is also strongly established here, running many events, including sessions for international visitors.

"The Sacred Heart of Jesus, pierced by our sins and for our salvation, is quite rightly considered the chief sign and symbol of that... love with which the divine Redeemer continually loves the eternal Father and all human beings without exception." (*Catechism of the Catholic Church* 478)

Saint Margaret Mary Alacoque

Margaret was born on 22nd of July 1647 in the village of L'Hautecour, Burgundy, the fifth child of seven. Her father was a local notary, and as such the family was well off. When she was eight her father died, and the family situation altered to one of enforced servitude to the domineering uncle and aunt, who had commandeered the family estate.

Soon after her father's death Margaret was dispatched to a convent to be educated. The nuns were impressed by her devout attitude and she received her First Holy Communion at the then early age of nine. No doubt they noticed that:

"Whenever I wanted to join in the games of my companions, I always felt something which called me and drew me aside into some little corner, leaving me no peace until I had followed it. Our Lord then made me give myself to prayer, and I did, almost always either prostrate or on my bare knees or making genuflections, provided nobody saw me, for it was strange torment to me when I was noticed. I also felt a great desire to do everything that I saw the nuns do, for I looked upon them all as saints and thought that, if I were a religious, I, too,

Saint Margaret Mary Alacoque.

should become one like them. This filled me with so great a longing that I thought of nothing else…".

Two years later Margaret fell ill with what is thought was rheumatic fever and eventually was sent home to recover. This short period at school was all she received by way of formal education. No medical cure seemed available, and it was only after prolonged suffering and in desperation that Margaret pledged to Our Lady she would become "one of her daughters", that she was instantly cured of this debilitating illness. "Scarcely had I made this vow, than I was cured, and taken anew under the protection of Our Lady".

One of the other aspects of Margaret Mary's early life that shines through very clearly and consistently, was her strong, determined devotion to the Blessed Sacrament. During the difficult years, when her family was oppressed by relatives, she was denied every opportunity to slip away to the local church to pray before Jesus in the Blessed Sacrament. She learned to overcome this by mentally prostrating herself before Jesus, maintaining her adoration through prayer 'at a distance'.

Vocation and consecration

When she was seventeen her brother came of age, the family regained their estate, and life improved again: but she was now beginning to come under the pressures of accepting proposals for a suitable marriage. In her words:

"For, on the one hand, my relations pressed me to accept; and my mother, incessantly weeping, told me that she looked to me as her only hope of putting an end to her misery by joining me as soon as I should be settled in the world, adding that this would be a great consolation to her. On the other hand, God pursued my heart so powerfully that I had no longer any peace, for not only was my vow constantly before my eyes, but I thought of the fearful torments which awaited me, if I should fail to keep it."

Whilst she may have toyed with the idea of marriage, there was always running through her life that vow that she mentions, made at a very early age: "Without knowing their meaning, I felt continually urged to pronounce the following words: 'O my God, I consecrate to You my purity, and I make You a vow of perpetual chastity'", and later, the realization of what that actually meant – a religious life consecrated to God.

So, resisting family pressures she entered the Visitation convent at Paray-le-Monial on 20th June 1671, aged twenty-four. On the day of entry she had severe misgivings, but as she crossed the threshold, "I understood that Our Lord had cut off the sackcloth of my captivity and was clothing me with His robe of gladness. In a transport of joy, I exclaimed: 'It is here that God wills me to be!'"

Although she treasured this Divine reassurance, the realities of convent life soon hit home when she realised that her mystical gifts and experiences would soon become the source of scepticism and even jealousy among her community: in that someone so young, and so inexperienced in the religious life, should be so gifted. She was obviously not in the expected, or accepted, 'mould' of a contemplative religious: "No matter how much I tried to practise what I was taught, I found it impossible to follow the method of prayer presented to me and was always constrained to return to my Divine Master, although I made every effort to forget all and turn away from Him".

Visions of the Sacred Heart

In the eighteen months starting on 27th December 1673, Margaret Mary began experiencing the amazing encounters with Christ that would clarify and specify her mission to the world – that of spreading the devotion to His Sacred Heart.

On this day, the Feast of St John the Evangelist, she was praying as usual before the exposed Blessed Sacrament in the convent chapel, when, "I felt myself wholly penetrated with that Divine Presence, but to such a degree that I lost all thought of myself and of the place where I was. He made me repose for a long time upon His Sacred Breast, where He disclosed to me the marvels of His love and the inexplicable secrets of His Sacred Heart".

Jesus told her:

"My Divine Heart is so inflamed with love for all, and for you in particular, that being unable any longer to contain within Itself the flames of Its burning love, It needs to spread them abroad by your means, and manifest Itself to all in order to enrich them with the precious treasures which I reveal to you, and which contain graces of sanctification and salvation necessary to withdraw them all from the abyss of perdition. I have chosen you as an abyss of unworthiness and ignorance for the accomplishment of this great design, in order that everything may be done by Me."

In her narrative of this supernatural event, Margaret Mary goes on:

"After this, He asked me for my heart, which I begged Him to take. He did so and placed it in His Adorable Heart, where He showed it to me as a little atom which was being consumed in this great furnace, and withdrawing it thence as a burning flame in the form of a heart. He restored it to the place whence He had taken it, saying to me, 'See, my well beloved, I give you a precious token of my love, having enclosed within your side a little spark of its glowing flames, that it may serve you for a heart and consume you to the last moment of your life; its ardour will never be exhausted, and you will be able to find some slight relief only by bleeding. As a proof of the great favour I have done you is not imagination, although I have closed the wound in your side, the pain will always remain. If hitherto, you have taken only the name of my servant, I now give you that of the beloved disciple of My Sacred Heart'."

For days after this encounter, Margaret Mary was barely able to restrain herself from crying out to all about her experience – but this she did, knowing that she had to exercise extreme caution in front of her community. From the time of this first revelation, on every first Friday of the month, she would suffer a recurrence of this burning pain in her side, up until her death.

Second and third revelations

The second revelation occurred some weeks after, early in 1674.

"The Divine Heart was presented to me in a throne of flames, more resplendent than a sun, transparent as crystal, with this adorable wound. And it was surrounded with a crown of thorns, signifying the punctures made in it by our sins, and a cross above signifying that from the first instant of His Incarnation, that is, as soon as the Sacred Heart was formed, the cross was implanted into it, and from the first moment it was filled with all the sorrow to be inflicted on it by the humiliations, poverty, pain, and scorn His Sacred humanity was to endure throughout His life and during His sacred Passion".

It was here that Jesus began to explain details of His intentions and promises. In Margaret Mary's words:

"This Heart of God must be honoured under the form of His Heart of flesh, whose image He wanted exposed, and also worn on me and on my heart. He promised to pour out into the hearts of all those who honour the image of His Heart all the gifts it contains in fullness, and for all those who would wear this image on their persons. He promised to imprint His love on their hearts and to destroy all unruly inclinations. Everywhere that this holy image was exposed to be honoured, He would pour forth His graces and blessings".

The third revelation took place in June 1674, again Margaret Mary was praying in front of the Blessed Sacrament, when Jesus appeared before her, "resplendent with glory, with His five wounds shining like five suns, and flames issuing from every part of His sacred humanity". It was on this occasion that He issued very precise instructions as to the devotions to the Sacred Heart, starting with: "I will be your strength, fear nothing, but be attentive to My voice and to what I shall require of you that you may be in requisite dispositions for the accomplishment of My designs.

In the first place, you shall receive Me in Holy Communion as often as obedience will permit you, whatever mortification or humiliation it may cause you, which you must take as pledges of My love. You shall, moreover, communicate on the first Friday of each month. Every night between Thursday and Friday I will make you share in the mortal sadness which I was pleased to feel in the Garden of Olives, and this sadness, without you being able to understand it, shall reduce you to a kind of agony harder to endure than death itself. And in order to bear Me company in the humble prayer that I then offered to My Father, in the midst of My anguish, you shall rise between eleven o'clock and midnight, and remain prostrate with Me for an hour, not only to appease divine anger by begging mercy for sinners, but also to mitigate in some way the bitterness which I felt at that time on finding Myself abandoned by My apostles, which obliged Me to reproach them for not being able to watch one hour with Me. During that hour you shall do what I shall teach you.

But listen, believe not lightly and trust not every spirit, for Satan is enraged and will seek to deceive you. Therefore do nothing without the approval of those who guide you; being thus under the authority of obedience, his efforts against you will be in vain, for he has no power over the obedient".

Passing on the messages

Of course, even the simple act of recounting and passing on these extraordinary experiences, let alone the demanding instructions of Our Lord, to her Superior and

Community were met with cynicism and doubt – particularly the very practical proposition of how an enclosed nun in a convent in the depths of rural France was going to spread this devotion to the rest of the world. It was only after a visible healing from a fever, asked for by her Superior as 'proof', did the Superior take positive action. A group of visiting theologians were invited to question Margaret Mary as to the credibility of her experiences: they declared her to be delusional, and that her visions were not from God.

The effect of this whole disheartening experience threw Margaret Mary into despair – doubting the reality herself, and suffering many temptations and crises of faith. She continued to suffer animosity of the most subtle form from individuals within her community. Margaret Mary herself admitted that some of the sisters used to throw holy water at her as if to exorcise her from evil spirits.

Jansenism

In wondering why, particularly in a religious community, such blatantly uncharitable actions were made against her, we need to consider one of the strongly prevailing theologies of the time – Jansenism. Jansenism was named after its principal proponent Cornelius Jansen (1585–1638) Bishop of Ypres, Belgium, and developed out of the Counter-Reformation and the aftermath of the

Council of Trent (1545–1563). Its main thrust at a philosophical and theological level was a strong emphasis on human nature being incapable of doing good, the denial of free will, and that only a minority of human beings were pre-destined by God for salvation.

At a practical level, this had the effect of increasing scrupulousness and self-mortification to a degree that obscured the wider considerations of acting and living within the loving spirit of the Gospel. Despite being condemned by Pope Innocent X in 1655 as heresy, it nonetheless continued as a strong influence right through to the 20th century. Someone like Margaret Mary was therefore probably viewed by members of her community as claiming, through her spiritual giftings, an assured place in God's salvific plan. They may also have strongly disapproved of the notion – which directly countered Jansenism – that she had found, and was joyfully talking of a God of unconditional love, forgiveness and compassion.

However, Our Lord had reassured Margaret Mary that he would send one of His servants to affirm and assist her with the task of spreading the devotion to His Sacred Heart. This came in the form of Father Claude de la Colombière, a Jesuit, assigned as confessor to the convent. As soon as they met, she heard the inner voice: "He it is I send you".

Father Claude, on his part, had no doubts as to the sanctity and sincerity of this young nun, believing without reservation the encounters she had experienced. Her Superior, respecting Father Claude's own reputation and discernment, was reassured, and instructed Margaret Mary – at last – to tell her confessor all. With Father Claude as confidant and supporter, her strength grew again in the belief and significance of her mission.

Fourth revelation

It was after meeting Father Claude that Margaret Mary had the fourth and final revelation from Jesus, in June 1675, during the octave of Corpus Christi. Here, Our Lord gave very specific instructions:

"I ask of you that the Friday after the Octave of Corpus Christi be set apart for a special Feast to honour My Heart, by communicating on that day and making reparation to It by a solemn act, in order to make amends for the indignities which It has received during the time It has been exposed on the altars. I promise you that My Heart shall expand Itself to shed upon those who shall thus honour It, and cause It to be honoured".

Subsequently, it was through Fr Claude with the respect and influence he had in the Church, and supported wholeheartedly by his Order – the Society of Jesus – that the devotion of the Sacred Heart was taken to every corner of the earth.

With a new Superior appointed in 1683, came a complete change of atmosphere and approach. Margaret

Mary was appointed Assistant Superior and placed in charge of the novitiate. With the tacit approval of her Superior she introduced the devotions to the Sacred Heart to her novices, and in 1686, on 21st June, the Feast of the Sacred Heart was celebrated by the whole community, from which it subsequently spread to more Visitandine and other religious houses throughout France, and of course now, throughout the world.

Death and canonisation

Having never been in the best of health for much of her life, she died, aged 43, in 1690, having served her community faithfully in the role of Assistant Superior and Novice Mistress. There seems to be no formal details of the illness to which she succumbed. The doctor who attended her is reported as saying that 'since she lived only for love, love was the cause of her death'. Before dying she uttered, "I have only the need of God, and the need of immersing myself in the Sacred Heart of Jesus". But more importantly, she died knowing that she had also faithfully and unswervingly served her beloved Lord's wish and instruction for the devotion to be instituted to His Most Loving and Sacred Heart.

As the Church requires, her writings, sayings and actions were examined minutely over a long period of time by the Sacred Congregation of Rites. In March 1824 Pope Leo XII declared her Blessed. In 1856 the Feast of the Sacred Heart was instituted as a universal Feast. In 1920 she joined the many, who, from the total obscurity of the cloister – sometimes following controversy and cynicism – initiated worldwide, popular devotions, and was canonised by Pope Benedict XV. Her feast day is celebrated throughout the Church on 16th October.

In the proclamation that the Holy See might safely proceed with the canonisation, Pope Benedict stated, "the pious daughter of St. Francis of Sales received from Jesus Himself the mission of making known the riches of His Divine Heart, that men might come to it as a fount of grace and model of virtue." He went on to add: "the historian may say today her story is complete; the theologian and canonist have carried their researches and examinations to the full length; from the hands of even the most critical the arms have fallen...there can be no room for delay in recognising the universal character of her apostolate."

Graces of the Sacred Heart

In issuing his Encyclical *Miserentissimus Redemptor*, which closely ties in the requirement for reparation with the Sacred Heart, Pope Pius XI stated, "There is surely no reason for doubting, Venerable Brethren, that from this devotion piously established and commanded to the whole Church, many excellent benefits will flow forth, not only to individual men, but also to society, sacred, civil, and domestic, seeing that our Redeemer Himself promised to Margaret Mary that 'all those who rendered this honour to His Heart would be endowed with an abundance of heavenly graces'."

In May 2006, Pope Benedict XVI, in a letter to the Superior General of the Jesuits on the 50th anniversary of the Encyclical *Haurietis Aquas* issued by Pope Pius XII, said that, "By encouraging devotion to the Heart of Jesus, the Encyclical *Haurietis Aquas* exhorted believers to open themselves to the mystery of God and of his love, and to allow themselves to be transformed by it. After 50 years, it is still a fitting task for Christians to continue to deepen their relationship with the Heart of Jesus, in such a way as to revive their faith in the saving love of God and to welcome him ever more fully into their lives."

St Claude de la Colombière.

Saint Claude de la Colombière

Claude de la Colombière was born in the Dauphine area of France around Grenoble, in the south east, on 2nd February 1641, some six years before Margaret Mary Alacoque. As with Margaret Mary, his father was also a notary, but the family was well connected with the French nobility and high society of the time. He led an extraordinary life of sanctity and virtue, and with hugely contrasting and contradictory circumstances, died of tuberculosis at the early age of 41.

A gifted man

He was clearly an intelligent, gifted and well-educated young man, much inclined to the arts and literature, with the prospect of an active and glittering social life. However, early on, he sensed a religious vocation, stating at one stage that he "had a terrible aversion for the life embraced". Aged seventeen he entered the Jesuit Novitiate in Avignon, where, after completing his studies and professing his first vows, he went on to become a professor of grammar and literature at the city's college. His growing reputation as a preacher was enhanced by the stirring sermon that he preached on the canonisation of St Francis de Sales in 1665. Whilst completing his studies in Paris, he had a short period as a personal tutor to the Minister of Finance. On completion of his studies, he returned to Avignon where he was appointed preacher to the college church, and where his reputation as such continued to grow.

In the lead-up to taking his final vows, aged thirty three – and seeing his life ahead of him at the same age at which Jesus was crucified – he pledged and consecrated himself to live by the strictest interpretation of the Jesuit Rule, avowing, "It seems right dear Lord, that I should begin to live in You, and for You alone, at the age at which You died for all, and for me in particular".

Appointment to Paray-le-Monial

In 1675, in a puzzling move made by his superiors, Father Claude was appointed Rector of the Jesuit college at Paray-le Monial – puzzling because Paray was a seeming backwater with little prospect or scope for his talents. However, this was the 'faithful servant and perfect friend' that Our Lord had promised Sister Margaret Mary, as part of his duties were spiritual director and confessor to the Visitation sisters in Paray.

After hearing Margaret Mary's anguish and turmoil over the reality and veracity of her mystical experiences – and through prayer and discernment – he realised the authenticity of it all. Thereafter he gave her every support and vowed to make every effort to affirm and spread the message of the Sacred Heart to the world.

Move to London

The power and endurance of this message, and his strong conviction over it, is further emphasised by the relatively short period that Fr Claude spent at Paray. For after only eighteen months, he was sent to London as tutor and preacher to Mary of Modena, Duchess of York, in 1676. He went knowingly and obediently into the potential political and spiritual minefield of the entangled and anguished state of Protestant England under the rule of Charles II, facing the future prospect of his heir, the then Duke of York and a Catholic, acceding to the throne. Fr Claude is reported as preaching and giving spiritual direction sensitively, but with no compromise. He certainly spoke publicly of the Sacred Heart, because subsequently Mary of Modena, as the then exiled Queen of England in France, petitioned the Holy See to establish a Feast in honour of the Sacred Heart, which was finally instituted in 1856.

He also received great consolation in those who came to him seeking reconciliation with the Catholic Church, stating, "I could write a book about the mercy of God I've seen Him exercise since I arrived here". It was also reported that because of the intensity of his work and the poor climate in London, evidence of pulmonary disease started to surface.

Exile

Just as suddenly and as briefly, his work at the Court of St James came to an abrupt end. In 1678 he was accused, in Titus Oates's fictitious revelations, of being party to a 'Popish plot' to assassinate Charles II. He was thrown into prison, and it was only through the direct influence of Louis XIV of France that he was released and exiled. He returned to France some weeks later, his health having suffered grievously from the grim prison conditions.

After a futile attempt for him to return to teaching in Lyon, he retired to Paray for the last two years of his life, where, in 1682, he died of a haemorrhage on 15th February. Sister Margaret Mary reassured the sisters the next day that there was now no need for prayers for Fr Claude, as, "He is now in a position to pray for us, so well placed is he in heaven by the goodness and mercy of the Sacred Heart of Our Lord". He was beatified by Pope Pius XI in 1929.

Canonisation

He was canonised by Pope John Paul II on 31st May 1992, at a ceremony during which he made this powerful summation: "The past three centuries allow us to evaluate the importance of the message which was entrusted to Claude de la Colombière . In a period of contrast between the fervor of some and the indifference or impiety of many, here is a devotion centred on the humanity of

Christ, on his presence, on his love of mercy and on forgiveness. The call to "reparation", characteristic of Paray-le-Monial, can be variously understood, but essentially it is a matter of sinners, which all human beings are, returning to the Lord, touched by his love, and offering a more intense fidelity in the future, a life aflame with charity. If there is solidarity in sin, there is also solidarity in salvation. The offering of each is made for the good of all. Following the example of Claude de la Colombière, the faithful understand that such a spiritual attitude can only be the action of Christ in them, shown through Eucharistic communion: to receive in their heart the Heart of Christ, and to be united to the sacrifice which he alone can offer worthily to the Father".

The Basilica of the Sacred Heart

This 11th century church was not dedicated specifically to the Sacred Heart until 1875, when Pope Pius IX raised it to the status of minor basilica in recognition of Paray-le-Monial becoming a centre for devotion to the Sacred Heart, after the beatification of Margaret Mary Alacoque in 1864. Indeed, being initially a priory church of the Benedictine community, it was not opened to public worship until 1794, the last monks having left Paray two years previously, when it was adopted by the town as the parish church. The church standing today is the third to occupy this site. The first monastery church (*Paray I*), endowed by Lambert, the Count of Chalon, was started in 973. It was subsequently enlarged and altered and consecrated in 1004 (*Paray II*) by the then Abbot, St Odilion. Not being satisfied with this, St Hugh the Great, Abbot of Cluny, and one of the driving forces at the time for the spread of the Cluniac monastic movement, ordered a rebuild, starting in 1092, of a church modelled on Cluny Abbey (*Paray III*). It was completed in the early 13th century.

Exterior

This handsome church is set in idyllic conditions overlooking the Bourbince and standing proud from the other buildings around it. It presents a prime and classic example of Romanesque architecture in the style of Cluny. As you stand at the front, looking up at the two, weathered, twin towers, you will soon realise that they are not actually 'twins'. You will notice that the left hand tower (northern) is a bit bolder and more refined in its architecture, certainly at the higher levels. It is in fact the more recent of the two, having been built between 1120 and 1130, whilst the southern tower is 11th century. To the right of the Basilica, directly abutting, is the substantial building making up the former monastery complex. It is through an arch, halfway down, that you may enter the small, neat and tranquil cloister garden, with its mediaeval planting, and also the southern portal of the church. Further round this building, to the extreme right and behind, are the remains of the 15th century original summer mansion of the Abbot of Cluny, with its blank-faced, robust, round tower, and conical, tiled 'hat'.

As you continue your wandering – clockwise from the frontage – you will take in the pale, irregular stonework, generally presenting a bluff and unadorned exterior. You will pass the oblong northern portal with its finely worked filigree carvings. Then, from this unassuming side aspect, and as you round the corner to the rear (east end) of the Basilica, you are in for a treat – for what you now see, when you stand back and examine the whole, is a tumbling, cascading, but well ordered architectural triumph of the

The interior of the Basilica of the Sacred Heart.

chevet (apse and apsidal area) at the eastern end! From the black-tiled, pointed steeple way up high, follows the series of descending circles, arches, pillars and windows, all forming as they descend: the end of the nave, the sanctuary and apse, the ambulatory, and finally the simple symmetric radiating apsidal chapels so typical of the Cluniac design. Emphasising and contrasting with this pale stoned, geometric visual descent are the warm red, semi-tubular rustic tiles, neatly capping each downward step.

Inside the Basilica

It is probably best to enter the church by going back to the main porched entrance from the riverside. Going in here will give the maximum effect of what immediately hit me: light and loft! Unlike many Romanesque churches, with their relatively small, high clerestory windows, this one is bright inside – mainly effected by the striking contrast between the bright butter-coloured pillars and arches and the plain, dazzling white walls and vaulted ceiling. Of course, sunlight, as it travels through and over this church during the day, also has a varying and dramatic effect, giving at times a lovely, soft interior luminosity to the church.

Then you see the huge loft and length of the building, and the march of pillars and arches as they take you down the seemingly endless long nave to the delicate sanctuary and apse, and the ambulatory beyond. The simple, plain, diamond-pattern flagged floor, in the same butter colour as the pillars, perfectly complements the whole. Modern chandeliers of brushed brass silhouettes of fish, fowl and foliage, woven with delicate black wrought-iron lily stalks, the bulbs placed discreetly in the delicately opening petals, add a touch of sophistication and drama.

Now take a wander round, clockwise – as suggested by the brochure available in the church. Note the large bronze statue of the seated St Peter – left rear – with his right foot wearing to the light patina caused by many thousands of touching hands. You will start to appreciate the complexity that gives the overall effect of simplicity and symmetry of the whole, as you examine the building from your walk down the left hand side-nave. The massive, granite holy water stoup just inside the transept entrance on your left (north porch) used to be a washbasin in the monastery. The first small side chapel that you see directly in front of you – just on the left of the north entrance – is the baptistery, with a beautiful, slender angel delicately pouring the baptismal waters into the font.

Going on round the ambulatory, you will come across the three perfectly formed and exquisitely executed side chapels – St Joseph's being the first (not the centre chapel as currently mentioned in the guide book) – ending with the right hand (southern) chapel dedicated to St Thérèse of Lisieux. Note the rather strange mermaid as the capital of one of the pillars in this chapel!

Sanctuary

As the guide booklet suggests, the delicate structures of the sanctuary area harmonize and illustrate what the building as a whole is trying to achieve. Notice up above you the large washed-out, distemper fresco, framed by an angular teardrop, and covering the whole, half-domed apse area, of Christ in His glory – holding the globe in His left hand and offering an Eastern-style blessing with His right hand. In each corner are the symbols of the Evangelists. This painting dates back to the late 15th century, but was only re-discovered and uncovered again in 1935.

To the right of the sanctuary, just outside the ambulatory, is a statue of St Margaret Mary Alacoque kneeling in prayer to the Sacred Heart of Jesus, and a large, modern, boat-shaped candle stand for votive candles.

Prayer of St Margaret Mary Alacoque

Lord Jesus,
let my heart never rest until it finds You,
who are its centre, its love, and its happiness.
By the wound in Your Heart
pardon the sins that I have committed
whether out of malice or out of evil desires.
Place my weak heart in Your own divine Heart,
continually under Your protection and guidance,
so that I may persevere in doing good
and in fleeing evil until my last breath. Amen.

Blessed Sacrament Chapel

To the right, in the south transept, is the Lady Chapel, in which resides the Blessed Sacrament. It is the only part of this building that is not Romanesque: it was added in the 15th century by a local notable family, in the style of a Gothic funeral chapel dedicated to St George. In it you will also note a powerful *Pietà* statue. A lovely quiet place to meditate and pray.

Meditation

Here is a powerful meditation, which although written in the late 19th century, sadly applies just as much – maybe more so – today:

Devotion to the Heart of our Divine Lord may be said to be the highest and most complete form of homage to His Sacred Humanity, inasmuch as it involves not only the worship of His material heart of flesh, but moreover, in a special manner, the worship of that divine love incarnate in his heart, which was the spring of every word and action of his life. Hence it is to the Heart of Our Blessed Lord, that are to be traced all those marvellous lessons of humility, submission, charity, and all other virtues of which his whole mortal career affords us so brilliant an illustration. In studying that heart, the great mystery of the Incarnation becomes clearer to us, and the means chosen by the Eternal for the redemption of the world, and manifested in Our

Lord Jesus Christ, break on us in a new light, indicating at the same time the only means by which society in the present day, the nations, the whole world, will find salvation from the evils that threaten the destruction of authority, of legitimate government, of subordination, both civil and religious – in a word, of all order, social and divine.

What then, are the tendencies characterising the devotion to the Heart of the Incarnate God? Before, and above all, submission. "Descendit de caelis... et homo factus est." Such was the first lesson imparted to men by Him who came to save them. He would teach them that the very foundation of all salvation should consist in and rest upon these two acknowledgements; the supreme sovereignty – the unlimited dominion of God, and, the absolute nothingness, and consequent utter dependence of the creature upon that infinite Being who alone is. From thence would flow obedience to his laws, submission to those representing his authority, and lastly, a spirit of subordination to all legitimately instituted power, inasmuch and as far as it was in harmony with the order of God...

If the sublime doctrine of the Heart of Jesus were more fully comprehended, and made to bear upon actual difficulties involving the gravest interests, how different an aspect would the world present at this hour. (*Fr Benedict Sestini SJ - d. 1890*)

Chapel of St Michael the Archangel

If you now go back down to the rear of the church, and if the small door on the back wall is open, go up to the upper bays of the 11th century porch. This is the Chapel of St Michael the Archangel, with its rough-hewn, exposed stonework of bays and arches, having been added on to 'Paray II' in 1075. A small notice in the chapel gives an interesting insight into one of its purposes: to pray for deceased monks, "30 Masses by six priests during thirty days after death, to help the dead man's soul reach Paradise". From the viewing arch in the chapel are stunning views of the Basilica laid out below you. The difference of orientation between 'Paray II' and 'Paray III' can be detected from here: if you stand with your back against the outer wall looking along the length of the church, you can see how this porch is slightly out of alignment with the 'new' church.

Other areas

Outside, and in the immediate vicinity of the Basilica, are other areas of interest. At the rear, just opposite the chevet, is the Pilgrim Information Office (*'Espace St Jean'*) in which you can request a viewing in English of the 25 minute dvd on the life and times of St Margaret Mary Alacoque. Also in this area is the well stocked pilgrim shop (very few publications in English), and just down by the side of the Basilica is the obliging Tourist Information Office.

The green cathedral

The other attractive and arresting area (probably more so in summer!) is the 'green cathedral'. This is behind the Basilica and fronted by the presbytery, denoted by the sign at the entrance gates as *'Parc des Chapelains'*. It is a large, grassed, park-like area – but as you will soon realise – with a difference. The numerous, tall, sizeable trees are planted in the pattern of a church, with a long, stately nave-like avenue leading up to the 'transept' area, in which stands the only stone feature of a dome, providing the sanctuary, with apse and altar. In it is a large, dramatic carved wooden crucifix scene, with St John taking Jesus down from the cross; it was presented by the Sisters of Bethlehem in 2009 for the Feast of the Sacred Heart. The trees – plane (or *platane*) – were planted in this pattern by some far-sighted person, in 1898. The cross-shape is quite explicit and visible when viewed from 'Google Earth' (as is the cloister garden)! There is extensive bench-seating for at least 2,000 – but full or empty, this is a lovely shady, cool, soothing space to be in, to either joyfully celebrate with others, or quietly meditate on your own.

Over on the left side is a low, shuttered entrance, in which you can view a diorama (entry free) of a well presented sequence of mini tableaux in sound and light, of the story of St Margaret Mary Alacoque. It is really quite charming, lasting about 20 minutes, with French commentary. Also round the perimeter of the green area are the Stations of the Cross, a dramatic grotto (on the left of the presbytery) of Jesus in Gethsemane. In front of the presbytery, you will not fail to notice the graceful statue of Our Lady, facing down the nave towards the altar, hands folded in prayer. At her feet is the most gorgeous display of neatly planted colourful flowers; behind her on a slight slope, is an exquisite, miniature sculpted box hedge in the shape of a heart, enclosing a profusion of bright scarlet flowers.

Meditation

If the weather is on your side, here is the perfect meditation, written by St Thérèse of Lisieux, for this prayerful place of nature:

Jesus deigned to teach me this mystery. He set before me the book of nature; I understand how all the flowers He has created are beautiful, how the splendour of the rose and the whiteness of the lily do not take away the perfume of the little violet or the delightful simplicity of the daisy. I understand that if all flowers wanted to be roses, nature would lose her springtime beauty, and the fields would no longer be decked out with little wild flowers.

And so it is in the world of souls, Jesus' garden. He willed to create great souls comparable to lilies and roses, but He has created smaller ones and these must be content to be daisies or violets destined to give joy to God's glances when He looks down at his feet. Perfection consists in doing His will, in being what He wills us to be.

The Chapel of the Visitation - apse fresco.

Chapel of the Visitation

A few hundred yards from the Basilica, tucked back from the rue de la Visitation, sits the small, convent Chapel of the Visitation (also known as the Chapel of the Apparitions). It was in this chapel that St Margaret Mary received the visions of Jesus and His Sacred Heart – the inscription above the entrance archway testifying to this: 'In this church Our Lord revealed His Heart to Saint Margaret Mary'. It is the focal point of the pilgrims' visit to Paray, as St Margaret Mary's mortal remains rest in a reliquary in this chapel, and from it, through Jesus' personal presence, emanated the modern devotion to His Sacred Heart.

The nuns of the Order of the Visitation of Holy Mary (Visitandines), co-founded by St Francis de Sales and St Jane de Chantal in Annecy in 1610, have been here – except for a short period following the French Revolution – since 1662. The monastery and chapel were built in 1662/3. In the aftermath of the Revolution in 1792 it was used as a dwelling place and warehouse, the sisters returning in 1823. The chapel was restored in 1856, and altered in 1926 to accommodate the small side chapel which houses the reliquary.

A simple chapel

The church retains the simplicity of its purpose – a monastery chapel for the sisters. It is solidly constructed with its squared pillars and understated, plain arched and vaulted ceiling. The predominant colours are warm browns, sienna and oranges, and the church is largely unadorned, emphasising its simplicity and liturgical purpose. The high, modern stained glass windows let in the light. It has a single, wide nave; on the left, a narrow side aisle leads up to a side altar dedicated to St Joseph. One of its notable and unusual devotional adornments is the Stations of the Cross, grouped closely together at the right rear of the church – each carved wooden Station depicting just the expression of Jesus' face.

When you enter and settle, your eye may be drawn immediately to the large fresco behind the altar, on the flat, arched wall of the apse. It depicts the vision of Jesus revealing His Heart to Margaret Mary. His arms are spread wide in the attitude of Crucifixion, His wounds glowing, but the centre-piece is His Heart, radiating and pulsating the intense Love that He so desires the world to experience and feel. Jesus is flanked, on His left, by Our Lady, St Paul, St Francis de Sales, St Jane de Chantal and Fr Mateo Crawley (Founder of the Sacred Heart Apostolate, and cured miraculously in this chapel in 1907); on His right are shown St John the Evangelist, St

Francis of Assisi, Blessed Charles de Foucauld, St John Eudes, and St Claude de la Colombière – all figures associated closely with the Sacred Heart or the life of St Margaret Mary. The mural was completed in 1966 by Luc Barbier.

In the sanctuary to the right and in front of the altar is the very beautiful, prominent, simple free-standing tabernacle. It comprises a large, gracefully curved and open silver heart, topped by a silver cross, the whole mounted on a slender, white marble block. At the front, the heart embraces the visible, red flame of the sanctuary lamp, and at the rear, through the unseen tabernacle door, the reserved Blessed Sacrament.

Reliquary

As you start to examine the chapel more closely, in the small brightly lit side chapel on the right near the altar rails, you will come across the reliquary of St Margaret Mary. The intricately gilded and shallow glass-fronted case, above the side altar, displays a full size, fully habited figure of St Margaret Mary, at rest and at peace. Her unseen relics are placed inside the reliquary. In the shallow arch above, is a bright, blazing, more abstract depiction of the Sacred Heart, surrounded by the Crown of Thorns, but through which pulsate the bright rays of Redemption. Carved above the arch is Jesus' promise to St Margaret Mary – 'I make you the heir to My Heart'.

A salutation prayer to the Sacred Heart by St Margaret Mary

Hail, Heart of Jesus, save me!
Hail, Heart of my Creator, perfect me!
Hail, Heart of my Saviour, deliver me!
Hail, Heart of my Judge, grant me pardon!
Hail, Heart of my Father, govern me!
Hail, Heart of my Spouse, grant me love!
Hail, Heart of my Master, teach me!
Hail, Heart of my King, be my crown!
Hail, Heart of my Benefactor, enrich me!
Hail, Heart of my Shepherd, guard me!
Hail, Heart of my Friend, comfort me!
Hail, Heart of my Brother, stay with me!
Hail, Heart of the Child Jesus, draw me to Thyself!
Hail, Heart of Jesus dying on the Cross, redeem me!
Hail, Heart of Jesus in all Your states, give Yourself to me!
Hail, Heart of incomparable goodness, have mercy on me!
Hail, Heart of splendour, shine within me!
Hail, most loving Heart, inflame me!
Hail, most merciful Heart, work within me!
Hail, most humble Heart, dwell within me!
Hail, most patient Heart, support me!
Hail, most faithful Heart, be my reward!
Hail, most admirable and most worthy Heart, bless me!

Inside the sanctuary and to the right you will see the large metal grille, through which the enclosed nuns of the Order can participate in Mass and other public liturgies. To the left, just off the sanctuary, is a side altar dedicated to Our Lady.

It is lovely to go to Mass here, encouraging to see the number of young people attending, uplifting to listen to the singing with gusto, peaceful joining the sisters for their daily liturgy, or just sitting, contemplating or praying during the quiet moments. There is a small shop attached to the chapel.

Meditation of the Sacred Heart

Before leaving this rather special place you may wish to quietly ponder this Meditation, so in tune with what Margaret Mary experienced. It was written by the French priest, St John Eudes, known chiefly for his promotion of the Immaculate Heart of Mary, but who had also already developed a private devotion to the Sacred Heart, by amongst other things, in about 1668, composing the Office of the Sacred Heart. It would also be appropriate to acknowledge here this forerunner and devotee to the Sacred Heart:

The most loving heart of our benign Saviour is a burning furnace of most pure love for us; a furnace of purifying love, of illuminating love, of sanctifying love, of transforming love, and of deifying love. His love is a purifying love, in which the hearts of holy souls are purified more perfectly than gold in the furnace; an illuminating love, which scatters the darkness of hell with which the earth is covered and lets us into the wonderful brilliance of heaven: "who has called you out of darkness into his marvellous light (1 *Pt* 2:9); a sanctifying love, which destroys sin in our souls in order to establish there the kingdom of grace; a transforming love, which transforms serpents into doves, wolves into lambs, beasts into angels, children of the devil into children of God, children of wrath and malediction into children of grace and blessing; a deifying love, which makes gods of men: "I have said: you are gods" (*Ps* 82:6), letting them share in the holiness of God, His mercy, His patience, His goodness, His love, His charity and His other divine perfections: "Partakers of the divine nature" (2 *Pt* 1:4). O divine love of my Jesus, I give myself wholly to you; purify me, enlighten me, sanctify me, transform me into you, that I may be naught but love for my God.

Adoration Chapel of Saint John

"The Church wishes to encourage ever greater numbers of the faithful to approach this Holy Sacrament with confidence so that their hearts may be ever more consumed in the flames of that divine charity which burned in the Sacred Heart of the Saviour when, in His infinite love, He instituted the Holy Eucharist." (*Pope Benedict XV*)

Above *Espace St Jean*, the Pilgrim Information Office, and accessed by the exterior staircase at the end of the building – by the prominent statue of the Sacred Heart – is the Chapel of St John, where non-stop Adoration – day and night – is conducted. It has a lovely, simple, barn-like interior, with plain white walls and apexed ceiling, exposed timbers and beams supporting the roof. (During silent hours you will need to obtain from the Pilgrim Office the access code for the door).

On a plain, plinthed, stone altar, is Our Lord in the brilliant, glittering throne of the monstrance, patiently awaiting our attendance… and our prayers… and our love. St Margaret Mary was rooted, from a very early age, to the devotion of the Blessed Sacrament. Here is our opportunity to go before the Lord with some sustained prayer.

Meditations in front of the Blessed Sacrament

Starting with a useful 'entry prayer' by Cardinal Newman:

O most sacred, most loving Heart of Jesus, Thou art concealed in the Holy Eucharist, and Thou beatest for us still. Now as then Thou sayest, "With desire I have desired." I worship Thee, then, with all my best love and awe, with my fervent affection, with my most subdued, most resolved will. O make my heart beat with Thy heart. Purify it of all that is earthly, all that is proud and sensual, all that is hard and cruel, of all perversity, of all disorder, of all deadness. So fill it with Thee, that neither the events of the day nor the circumstances of the time may have power to ruffle it; but that in Thy love and Thy fear it may have peace.

Followed by these beautiful thoughts from St Thérèse of Lisieux:

I need a heart burning with tenderness,
Who will be my support for ever,
Who loves everything in me, even my weakness…
And who never leaves me day or night.
I could find no creature
Who could always love me day or night.

I could find no creature
Who could always love me and never die.
I must have a God who takes on my nature
And becomes my brother and is able to suffer!

You heard me, only Friend whom I love.
To ravish my heart, you became man.
You shed Your blood, what a supreme mystery!

O Heart of Jesus, treasure of tenderness,
You Yourself are my happiness, my only hope.
You who knew how to charm my tender youth,
Stay near me till the last night…

Ah! I know well, all our righteousness
Is worthless in your sight.
To give value to my sacrifices,
I want to cast them into Your Divine Heart.
You did not find Your angels without blemish.
In the midst of lightning You gave Your law!...
I hide myself in Your Sacred Heart, Jesus.
I do not fear, my virtue is You!

Our Lord's twelve promises

In this quiet sanctuary, in the Presence of Our Lord, it may also be a suitable occasion to contemplate the twelve promises made by Our Lord to St Margaret Mary. The promises will be fulfilled to those who honour the Sacred Heart by making a Novena of nine Holy Communions on nine successive first Fridays of the month, with the right dispositions, and especially with the intention of making reparation to the Heart of Jesus for one's own sins and sins committed by others:

- I will give them all the graces necessary for their state of life.
- I will establish peace in their homes.
- I will comfort them in all their afflictions.
- I will be their secure refuge during life, and especially at the hour of death.
- I will bestow abundant blessings on all their undertakings.
- Sinners shall find in my Heart the source and ocean of infinite mercy.
- Tepid souls shall become fervent.
- Fervent souls shall rise rapidly to a high degree of perfection.
- I will bless every place where a picture of my Sacred Heart shall be exposed and honoured.
- I will give to priests the power to touch the hardest hearts.
- Those who shall promote this devotion shall have their names written in my Heart, never to be blotted out.
- I promise you, in the excessive mercy of my Heart, that its all-powerful love will grant to all those who receive Holy Communion on the First Friday of every month for nine consecutive months, the grace of final repentance, and that they shall not die without receiving the sacraments, and that my Divine Heart shall be their safe refuge in that last moment.

Act of Consecration to the Sacred Heart

O Sacred Heart of Jesus -
Fully acknowledging my weaknesses and lack of consistent resolve, I passionately desire to consecrate and offer up my person and my life to You: all my actions, trials, sufferings, triumphs and joys, so that my entire being may from now on be only used in loving, honouring and glorifying You.

I fully realise the challenges in trying to attain this, but this is my ardent yearning, to belong entirely to You, and to do all for Your love, renouncing with my whole heart all that can displease You. I pray You give me the grace to achieve and maintain this desire, the awareness to recognise when I am in default, and the strength to regain and re-implement my desire.

I wish to take You, O Most Precious Heart, as the sole object of my love, the protection of my life, the pledge of my salvation, the remedy of my frailty, the answer to my inconstancy, the reparation for the defects of my life, and my secure refuge at the hour of my death.

O Most Merciful Heart, I beg You to intercede with God Our Father, seeking His loving forgiveness for all my wrongdoings. I fear all from my own weakness and willfulness, but confidently place my entire confidence and trust in You, O Heart of Love. I hope all from Your infinite Goodness. Obliterate in me all that can displease or defy You. Imprint Your pure love so deeply into my own heart that I may never forget You or be separated from You.

I implore You, through Your infinite Goodness, that my name be engraved upon Your Heart, for in Your Heart I place all my happiness and all my glory, to live and to die as one of Your devoted servants. Amen.

Most Sacred Heart of Jesus, we place all our trust in You.
Most Sacred Heart of Jesus, we place all our trust in You.
Most Sacred Heart of Jesus, we place all our trust in You.

Chapelle la Colombière

A short walk on from the Chapel of the Visitation, in a quiet corner of the town, is the church dedicated to St Claude de la Colombière, in which his relics reside. Its rather conventional, pale-stoned exterior, dominated by the green conical copper dome with a large statue of the Sacred Heart of Jesus topping it, completely belies what lies inside! My first impression on entering – demonstrating my complete lack of architectural literacy – was: what a busy and confusing looking church! Smooth, round, brown-streaked marble pillars, topped with polychromed, bas-relief capitals, interspersed by angular pink and white striped brick pillars and arches, the whole topped by a diagonally laid redbrick effect semi-domed roof, and underpinned by a dizzying, patterned, pink, white and black mosaic floor! There did not seem to be any architectural symmetry or unity at all. But... on being confronted by such seeming confusion, I employed my standard tactic – slow down – sort it out – bit by bit! And in doing just that, I soon began to realise what an intriguing and beguiling church this is – a real treat, and one which really catches the imagination.

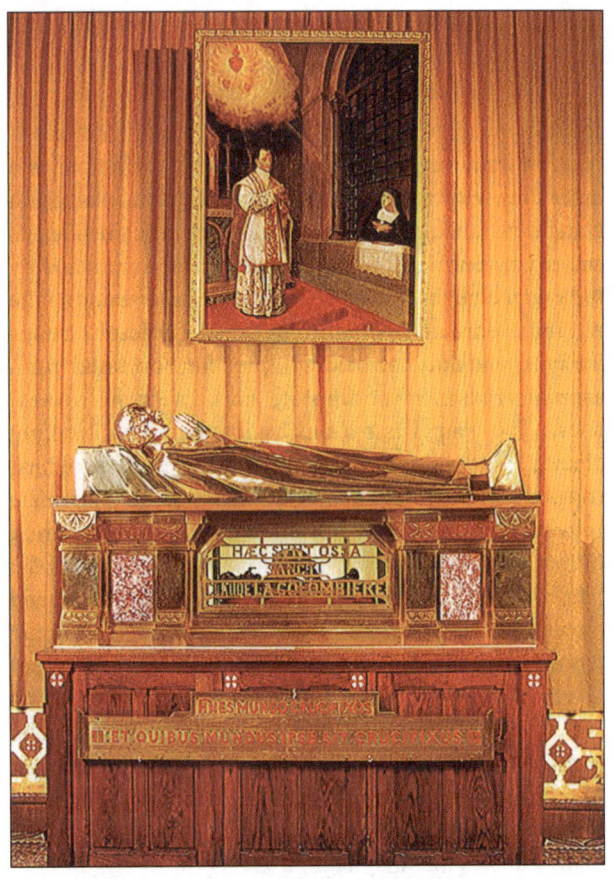

The Chapel and relics of St Claude de la Colombière.

Jesuit chapel

Recognisable, from exterior by its prominent *IHS* 'logo', is that this is a Jesuit chapel, being built in 1929 by the Jesuit community to celebrate Claude de la Colombière's beatification. It is described as being of Byzantine inspiration. Before examining it in detail it may be worth going down the nave to the left-hand transept side chapel, and paying one's respects to St Claude. Atop the reliquary is the graceful, recumbent figure of St Claude in soft, rich, gleaming brass, hands joined in prayer. Beneath that, in the brass and pink-marbled reliquary, his bones and skull, are plainly visible. The reliquary sits on a simple wooden chest. The chapel is backed by a tasteful, full length, pleated, gold-coloured curtain, in the middle of which hangs the classic picture of St Margaret Mary, behind the convent grille, about to receive Holy Communion from St Claude, and above whom burns the flaming furnace of the Sacred Heart. I found this a very simple, dignified and moving setting in which to quietly and reflectively pray this prayer of St Claude:

An Act of Hope and Confidence in God

My God, I believe most firmly that You watch over all who hope in You, and that we can want for nothing when we rely upon You in all things; therefore I am resolved for the future to have no anxieties, and to cast all my cares upon You.

People may deprive me of worldly goods and of honours; sickness may take from me my strength and the means of serving You; I may even lose Your grace by sin; but my trust shall never leave me. I will preserve it to the last moment of my life, and the powers of hell shall seek in vain to wrestle it from me.

Let others seek happiness in their wealth, in their talents; let them trust to the purity of their lives, the severity of their mortifications, to the number of their good works, the fervour of their prayers; as for me, O my God, in my very confidence lies all my hope. "For You, O Lord, singularly has settled me in hope." This confidence can never be in vain. "No one has hoped in the Lord and has been confounded."

I am assured, therefore, of my eternal happiness, for I firmly hope for it, and all my hope is in You. "In You, O Lord, I have hoped; let me never be confounded."

I know, alas! I know but too well that I am frail and changeable; I know the power of temptation against the strongest virtue. I have seen stars fall from heaven, and pillars of firmament totter; but these things alarm me not. While I hope in You I am sheltered from all misfortune, and I am sure that my trust shall endure, for I rely upon You to sustain this unfailing hope.

Finally, I know that my confidence cannot exceed Your bounty, and that I shall never receive less than I have hoped for from You. Therefore I hope that You will sustain me against my evil inclinations; that You will protect me against the most furious assaults of the evil one, and that You will cause my weakness to triumph over my most powerful enemies. I hope that You will never cease to love me, and that I shall love You unceasingly. "In You, O Lord, have I hoped; let me never be confounded." Amen.

Mosaics

Have a look now at the truly splendid, vibrant apse mosaic: the enthroned Jesus, arms open, in a gesture encompassing the four principal figures around him – St Francis de Sales, St Claude, St Margaret Mary and Our Lady. The whole group is surrounded by angelic, winged figures, and blazing rays strike out into the cobalt blue beyond. A dramatic gold and blue stairway ascends to Jesus through the clouds below. The high altar is fabulous – white/grey streaked marble, fine, inlaid mosaic panels – underneath the altar, deer drinking from the Living Water. The tabernacle door picks out in mosaic the beautiful, serene face of Jesus, eyes heavenward, offering His Sacred Heart to the Father. Finally, just examine the intricate mosaic and marble geometric patterns decorating the foot of the apse. In all, a powerful inspiring, harmonious compilation of art and fine workmanship, giving all glory to God.

At each side of the apse are two side altars, depicting the missionary apostolate of the Jesuits, and in the same vivid mosaic style. On the left – St Francis Regis converting and evangelising in Europe, and on the right – St Francis Xavier baptising in Japan.

The serving altar stands beneath the dome in the centre of the shallow transept. The dome ceiling is of blue and gold mosaic chips; light streams in from sixteen stained glass windows of angelic figures, set in the short octagonal tower that supports the dome. On the right transept is a simple, yellow marbled side altar, dedicated to St Joseph, whose statue the carpenter/worker is above, and to the side is a statue of St Ignatius Loyola.

Walking back down the church, look up at the organ gallery, where you will see the rear, triple windows of the Crucifixion, dramatically and effectively split by the organ pipes – and if the moment is right, a blaze of glory when the sun shines through! Also left rear, as you face the exit, an exquisite, long-apsed side chapel, effectively pierced by stained glass windows, the apse showing St Magdalene de Pazzi praying to St Aloysius Gonzaga. To me this lovely collage of glass and mosaic, in this miniature chapel, summed up perfectly this extraordinary place of worship.

Meditation

Sitting in this quiet church you may wish to reflect on Saint Claude's thoughts on God's mercy:

What does amaze me is that God should be so affected when we stray. He knows quite well that we are nothing, and suffers no real loss when we break away from him. Yet he shows profound grief at our separation and makes every effort to win us back. Nor is that mere fantasy; it is the teaching of the Gospel and of Jesus Christ himself.

Would you care to know what the Saviour of the world feels every time you lose the grace of God? He is distressed to the very depths of his soul; he is as troubled as a poor shepherd who has lost one of his sheep, or a poor woman who mislays one of the ten gold coins that are all her worldly wealth. The Son of God uses these two comparisons to make us understand his own sorrow at losing us.

Imagine the desolation of the poor shepherd whose sheep has gone astray. The entire countryside resounds with the cries of the unfortunate man; neglecting the rest of his flock, he runs through woods and over hills, combing thickets and undergrowth, lamenting and shouting at the top of his voice. He cannot bring himself to give up until he has found his lost sheep and brought it back to the fold. That is how the Son of God acted. When disobedient humanity had escaped from the Creator's guidance, the Son of God came down to earth and spared neither toil nor trouble to restore us to the position from which we had fallen. He still does the same thing daily for those who have strayed from him through sin. He follows their trail, so to speak, calling them again and again until he succeeds in getting them back on the road to salvation. And indeed, if he had not taken such care of us, our fate, as you know, would have been sealed after the first mortal sin. We could never have recovered from it. It is he who must make all the advances, who must offer us his grace, pursue us and beg us to take pity on ourselves; otherwise we should never think of asking him for mercy.

God's ardour in pursuing us is no doubt born of his very great mercy. But the gentleness with which he exercises that zeal shows an even more wonderful kindness. Despite his intense desire to win us back he never uses force, but only the gentlest of ways. I find no sinner in the entire Gospel story who was induced to repent by anything other than gentleness and kindness.

Final thoughts

The messengers

Before concluding specifically on our thoughts on the Sacred Heart and Paray-le-Monial, it may be worth musing briefly over the 'messengers' that God uses, and to whom He also seemingly issued the impossible task in requiring the message to be successfully delivered. I am thinking particularly of that group of the enclosed and cloistered nun. We have already seen how the seemingly impossible task given to Margaret Mary was accomplished – but she was not a 'one off' – for joining her in subsequent centuries, and also successfully delivering messages of some consequence and content, also in the face of opposition and adversity, were two other nuns - St Thérèse of Lisieux (1873-1897) and St Faustina Kowalska (1905-1938).

In the cases of St Margaret Mary and St Thérèse, they were both in total enclosure, only seeing the outside world through the convent grille, or on a rare visit to a doctor or dentist; and only hearing about it, usually through the limited, but very authentic filter of a prayer request. The Polish nun, Saint Faustina, who Our Lord used as His advocate to spread the message of the Divine

Mercy, although not totally enclosed, lived in the relative isolation of pre-Second World War Poland.

Although two centuries apart, the parallels between Margaret Mary and Thérèse are striking. Both French, both lost a parent at an early age, both were healed of debilitating childhood illnesses through the intercession of Our Lady, both had mystical experiences at very early ages, and both had the strong desire to dedicate their lives to God from the anonymity of the enclosure – yet both achieved world-wide exposure and recognition of their apostolate, receiving the crown of sainthood in the process. The difference is that Margaret Mary received very precise and detailed instruction personally from Jesus, and was reassured that a 'friend and servant' would be found to assist her. Faustina, similarly, had very precise instructions from Jesus about the content of the Divine Mercy. Thérèse on the other hand had no such assurances or specific instruction – just a huge desire to live a child-like life of Love, to become a missionary during her life on earth, and, after she had passed on, to spend her 'heaven doing good on earth'.

Delivery of the message

St Margaret Mary's mission was taken on, as we have heard, by that 'friend and servant', her confessor, St Claude de la Colombière, who took it to the outside world, and latterly the Jesuits corporately took on this task, which they, and a number of other Apostolates and individuals, continue to do to this day. Thérèse's mission only emerged after her death, through a growing popular recognition by the faithful of the powerful message in her autobiography, *Story of a Soul*, accompanied by many conversions and miracles for those who sought her intercession. Through her relics, which have visited over forty-six countries of the world, including this country, she still continues to deliver God's message to millions of people.

But all three, Margaret Mary, Thérèse and Faustina, had struggles and setbacks in getting the message believed and propagated, - either from their own community (in the case of Margaret Mary and Thérèse), or the Vatican (Margaret Mary and Faustina). All met with scepticism and jealousy when such supernatural encounters were evaluated. The fact that they all died relatively young (Thérèse and Faustina from tuberculosis) may seem immaterial. It was the delivery of the message that was important.

The underlying conclusion seems to be that despite the human barriers and resistance put up in denying these devotions their rightful place amongst the faithful, and against all human odds, they have been strongly established and rooted, and continue through the perseverance and trust of those faithful adherents. And when one further widens the field to those other humble messengers – the children – such as St Bernadette, the visionaries of Pontmain, the seers of Fatima, this paradox of their lowly origin can only strengthen and authenticate their divine source. For that is how Jesus, Our Sovereign Lord and King, emerged to the world – as a vulnerable baby, born in a stable to a lowly family – but emerging to deliver the most powerful message and promise for humankind.

The evocations of Paray

The lovely thing about reading about or – better still – going to Paray-le-Monial, is that because of its very 'ordinariness' there are no major distractions if you are there on pilgrimage – or even just visiting – but in some, maybe even undefined way, seeking out the Sacred Heart. The holy buildings and places are perfectly keyed to help facilitate your search, again without undue distraction. The other striking thing, is that by virtue of the very humble and low profile that St Margaret Mary adopted, there are no strong personality cult distractions. The way – on all fronts – is completely clear to focus totally on Jesus, and His Sacred Heart.

The simple, dignified, bright Basilica, dedicated to the Sacred Heart, gives us that vast soaring space and a delicate beauty, one created by human hands with love and labour, one in which prayers have resonated over the centuries, one around which to slowly wander, or to kneel, and to contemplate and give thanks for the wonders and gifts of the Father.

That small intimate, prayerful Chapel of the Visitation, still steeped in quiet but powerful prayer by the faithful nuns of today, as it was in Margaret Mary's time, over three hundred years ago. A place graced specifically with Our Lord's presence, inspiring us to bring to our mind those powerful images of the purifying flames from the furnace of Love of the Sacred Heart of the Son, aided by the vibrant image of the apse fresco. And quietly resting there, the mortal remains of his faithful messenger, St Margaret Mary Alacoque.

Then that magnificent 'green cathedral' – nature crafted by human hands – giving that peace and tranquillity, accompanied, in the quiet moments, just by the soughing of the wind and soft rustle of the leaves, bringing to one's awareness soft whisperings – the gentle presence of the Holy Spirit.

The Adoration Chapel of St John, being faithfully served, day and night, by local people, and being joined by those pilgrims and travellers – like us – who want to escape for a few quiet moments, and contemplate, on the altar, the Real Presence of Jesus, and to consecrate ourselves afresh to His Sacred Heart.

Lastly, the dynamic glory of the Chapel of St Claude de la Colombière, reminding us of this other dedicated, understated person, and also of today's Jesuits and other apostolates and individuals, who toil with such faith and trust in propagating the devotion to the Sacred Heart. We pray that they may continue in their unstinting efforts in a noisy and ignoring world.

Finally, I would like to leave you with this modern Meditation, which gathers up the strands and thoughts of your 'virtual' or actual visit to Paray, providing a brilliant summary as to what the Sacred Heart is all about. The phrase striking me most powerfully was that Jesus' Heart was 'forced open by the vehemence' of His love, when the Roman soldier speared Him as He hung on the Cross:

Final meditation

The object of devotion to the Sacred Heart is, properly speaking, the physical Heart of Jesus which is worthy of adoration, because it is part of His sacred humanity, hypostatically united to the Word. However, the ultimate object of this devotion is the love of Jesus, the symbol of which is His Heart. In other words:

"beneath the symbolic image of the Heart, we contemplate and venerate our Divine Redeemer's immense charity and generous love" (Pius VI). This is the real meaning of the devotion to the Sacred Heart by which the Church asks us to honour the Heart of Jesus as the visible representation of His invisible love...

His divine love becomes sensible, comprehensible and tangible to us by means of the manifestations of His human love. It is always the humanity of Jesus which reveals His divinity to us, and just as we know the Son of God through His sacred humanity, so do we know His divine love through the human love of Jesus…

"We too, pilgrims in the flesh, love as much as we can, and embrace the One who was wounded for us, whose hands, feet, side and Heart were pierced. Let us love and pray: 'O Jesus, deign to bind our hearts, still so hard and unrepentant, with the chain of Your love and wound them with its dart'" (*St Bonaventure*).

"O Jesus, a soldier opened your side with his lance, so that, through the gaping wound, we might know the charity of your Heart, which loved us unto death, and that we might enter into your unutterable love through the same channel by which it came to us.

Approach, then, O my soul, the Heart of Christ, that magnanimous Heart, that hidden Heart, that Heart which thinks of all things and knows all things; that loving Heart, all on fire with love. Make me understand, O Lord, that the door of your Heart was forced open by the vehemence of your love. Allow me to enter into the secret of that love which was hidden from all eternity, but is now revealed by the wound in your Heart" (*St Bernadine of Siena*). (*Fr Gabriel of St Mary Magdalen - d. 1952 OCD*)

Informative Catholic Reading

We hope that you have enjoyed reading this booklet.

If you would like to find out more about CTS booklets - we'll send you our free information pack and catalogue.

Please send us your details:

    Name ....

    Address ....

    ....

    ....

    Postcode ....

    Telephone ....

    Email ....

Send to: CTS, 40-46 Harleyford Road,
               Vauxhall, London
               SE11 5AY

Tel: 020 7640 0042
Fax: 020 7640 0046
Email: info@cts-online.org.uk

CTS